Stringtastic
BOOK 1: TEACHER'S ACCOMPANIMENT

Mark Wilson and Paul Wood
With illustrations by Sarah-Leigh Wills

For online backing tracks scan the QR code
or go to fabermusic.com/audio

FABER *ff* MUSIC

Contents

All music and lyrics by Mark Wilson and Paul Wood unless otherwise stated. With thanks to our editor, Emily Bevington.

The rights of Mark Wilson and Paul Wood to be identified as the joint authors of this work, and of Sarah-Leigh Wills to be identified as the creator of page illustrations in this work, have been asserted in accordance with the Copyright, Designs and Patents Act, 1988.

© 2022 by Faber Music Ltd
First published by Faber Music Ltd
Bloomsbury House, 74–77 Great Russell Street, London WC1B 3DA
Music processed by Donald Thomson
Cover design by WattGenius Creative
Page design by Chloë Alexander
Page illustrations by Sarah-Leigh Wills
Printed in England by Caligraving Ltd
All rights reserved

ISBN10: 0-571-54259-X
EAN13: 978-0-571-54259-8

To buy Faber Music publications or to find out about the full range of titles available please contact your local music retailer or Faber Music sales enquiries:

Faber Music Ltd, Burnt Mill, Elizabeth Way, Harlow CM20 2HX
Tel: +44 (0) 1279 82 89 82
fabermusic.com

Learn as you play through the world of *Stringtastic!*

Stringtastic Book 1 is an exciting collection of fun new compositions covering a wide range of styles. These pieces are progressively presented, taking the player on a journey from the D major scale through to Grade 1 (Early Elementary) level. No more than one technique is introduced at a time and space is given for consolidation.

These books have been designed for maximum flexibility:

- *Stringtastic Book 1* for violin, viola, cello and double bass is fully integrated to work together in any combination – ideal for use in individual lessons as well as group lessons and string orchestras.

- Many tunes have fun lyrics to sing, helping to develop a strong sense of pitch and rhythm. Learners can try writing their own lyrics, too!

- Dynamics are given throughout, but players are encouraged to add their own once a confident sound has been developed. Where there are lyrics, dynamics have consistently been placed below the lyric line.

- Fingering varies across the instrumental books but all is discretionary and flexible.

- While there are 57 pieces in total, eight of these are equal-level duets, both accompanied and unaccompanied; here players are encouraged to learn both parts.

- Instrumental cues are given throughout. Where instrumental lines differ from the violin part, the cello cue has been provided by default. For clarity, the use of the alto (viola) clef has been avoided.

- Some instrumental parts and accompaniments are deliberately written in different keys (pieces 8, 43 and 44) to avoid accidentals in the instrumental parts that could detract from the learning at that stage.

- Every tune has a fun backing track to play along to, as well as a piano-only backing track for practice:

Scan the QR code or go to fabermusic.com/audio to download the tracks.

Hi, I'm Spot the Cat!

And I'm Dotty Dog!

1. Time for C!

Time for C, then it's B, A and B and then it's C!

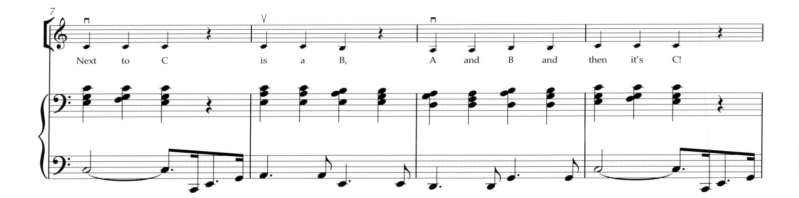

Next to C is a B, A and B and then it's C!

Nice and stea - dy, play with me.

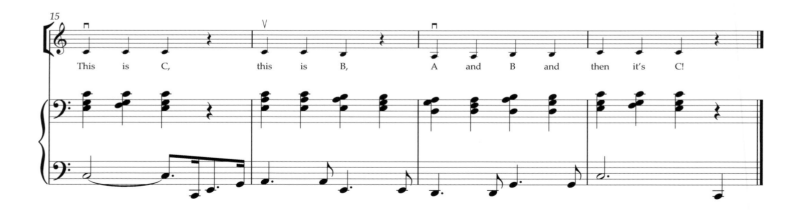

This is C, this is B, A and B and then it's C!

© 2022 by Faber Music Ltd.

2. Deep feelings

© 2022 by Faber Music Ltd.

3. Gee up!

Simply ♩ = 84—120

All

There's noth-ing quite like the sound of low notes, come on and let us sing!

Make sure your bow arm is at the right height, so our string can ring!

C, C, B, A, A, B, C, C, B, A, B, A, G, G!

You'll have such fun play-ing low notes like me, we make a rich, warm sound.

Smile as you play all us love-ly low notes; with a sound so round!

© 2022 by Faber Music Ltd.

4. Welly Bob shuffle

© 2022 by Faber Music Ltd.

5. Boogie bow

© 2022 by Faber Music Ltd.

6. C air

© 2022 by Faber Music Ltd.

7. Into the deep C

© 2022 by Faber Music Ltd.

8. Bassers and chasers

N.B. The key signature in the instrumental parts
has been deliberately omitted.

© 2022 by Faber Music Ltd.

9. City of dust

© 2022 by Faber Music Ltd.

10. Listen

Happily ♩ = 96—116

© 2022 by Faber Music Ltd.

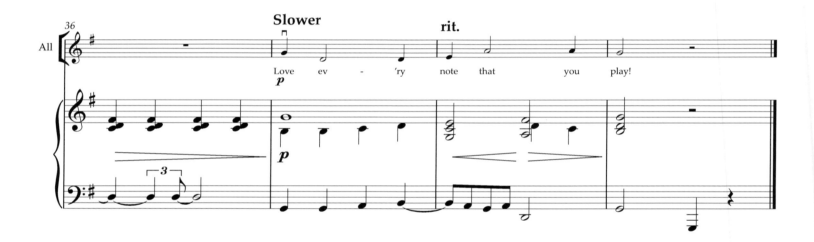

11. Flowing downstream

© 2022 by Faber Music Ltd.

12. Happy and free

© 2022 by Faber Music Ltd.

Play all these notes as they fall and they rise, look a-head so noth-ing is a sur - prise.

E and then F sharp, fol-lowed by E, climb to the top, feel-ing hap-py and free.

Look at the shape that the notes make, fol-low your mu - sic and you will sound great!

13. Be a butterfly

© 2022 by Faber Music Ltd.

14. When the world has gone to sleep

© 2022 by Faber Music Ltd.

15. A hint of jasmine

© 2022 by Faber Music Ltd.

16. Smoothly does it

Smoothly ♩ = 88   **Theme: Full bows**

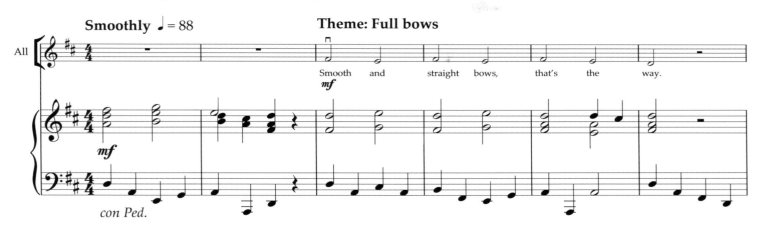

Smooth and straight bows, that's the way.

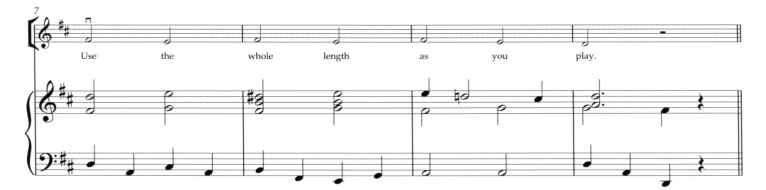

Use the whole length as you play.

Variation 1: Broken slurs

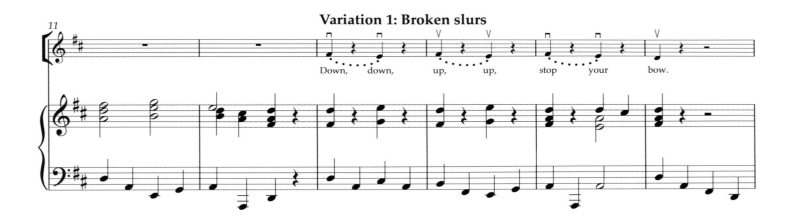

Down, down, up, up, stop your bow.

Best to play this nice and slow.

© 2022 by Faber Music Ltd.

Variation 2: Slurs

Down bow, up bow, here we go!

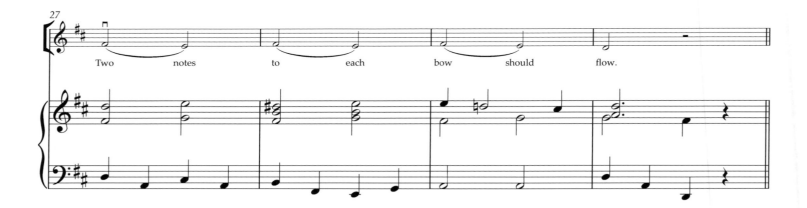

Two notes to each bow should flow.

Variation 3: Slurs and separates

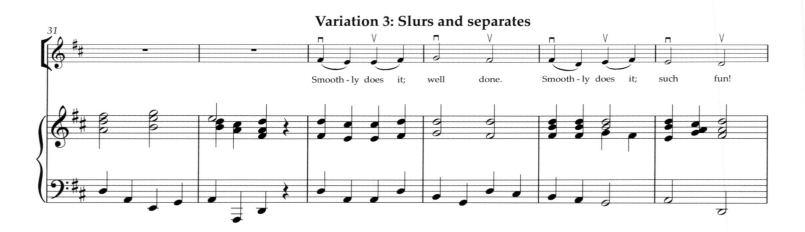

Smooth - ly does it; well done. Smooth - ly does it; such fun!

rit.

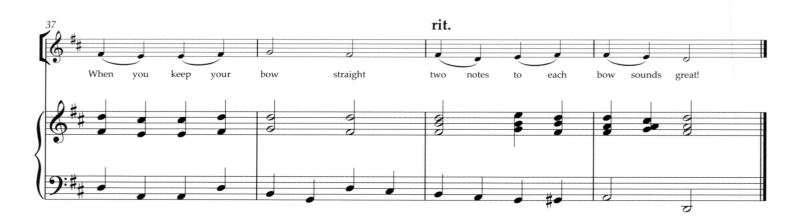

When you keep your bow straight two notes to each bow sounds great!

17. Blue sky

© 2022 by Faber Music Ltd.

18. Sometimes

© 2022 by Faber Music Ltd.

wan - d'ring in worlds far a - way.

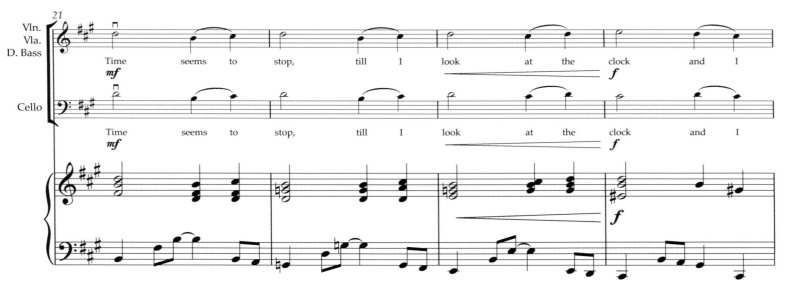

Vln.
Vla.
D. Bass

Time seems to stop, till I look at the clock and I

Cello

Time seems to stop, till I look at the clock and I

D.S. al Coda*

All

see that I've played all the day.

⊕ CODA   **rit.**

All

play. Where do I stray? Who can say?

* N.B. This instruction is D.C. al Coda in the instrumental parts.

19. Sticky toffee pudding

© 2022 by Faber Music Ltd.

20. Clever cat

With *feline!* ♩ = 66—84

© 2022 by Faber Music Ltd.

21. Come and play with us

© 2022 by Faber Music Ltd.

22. Dotty's dotted notes

Rhythmically ♩ = 76—88

mf

All

Look at Dot - ty danc-ing to the rhy-thm of our dot - ty dot - ted notes!

Spot just loves to lis-ten to the sound we make as through the air it floats.

Dot - ted notes are real - ly ea - sy, I'm sure you'll a - gree.

1, 2, 3, 4, 1 & 2 & 3 & 4 & 1 (2) & 3 (4) & 1 (2, off).

© 2022 by Faber Music Ltd.

23. Playtime

Happily ♩ = 76—88

All

Spin and jump and feel the rhy-thm of the mu - sic. Dance and twirl and move your bo - dy to the beat.

Laugh and smile and fill the world with joy-ful sing - ing. Play and sway and lis-ten to the love-ly sound you

make! So come on, let's play!

© 2022 by Faber Music Ltd.

24. Quiver of eighths

Flighty ♩. = 54—76

© 2022 by Faber Music Ltd.

25. Higgledy-piggledy

© 2022 by Faber Music Ltd.

26. Ducks on a pond

© 2022 by Faber Music Ltd.

27. Hide-and-seek

N.B. **28. Jig Together** is unaccompanied.

© 2022 by Faber Music Ltd.

29. Dark forest

© 2022 by Faber Music Ltd.

30. Four great friends

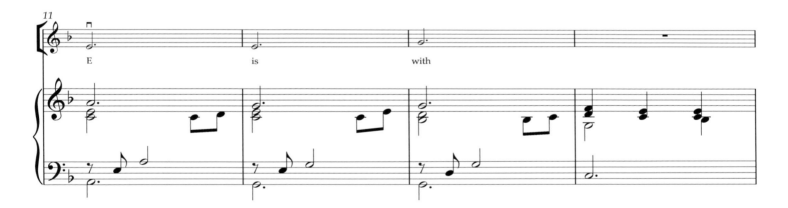

© 2022 by Faber Music Ltd.

31. Bullfrog rant

© 2022 by Faber Music Ltd.

Long and short, big and fat,

p

p

jui - cy flies in my tum - my! Yes, we can have some fun,

f

f

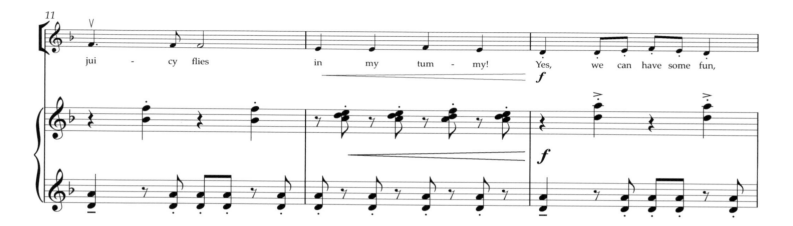

you, me and ev - 'ry - one, just danc - ing in the sun.

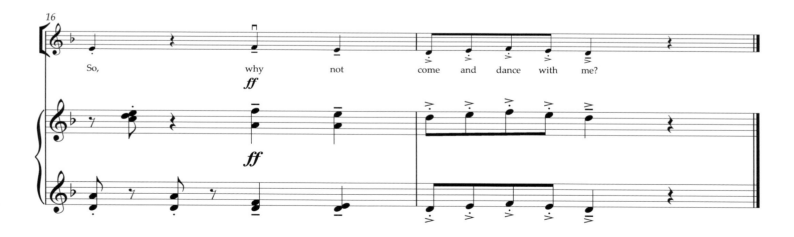

So, why not come and dance with me?

ff

ff

32. Come, let's dance!

Flowing ♩ = 116

© 2022 by Faber Music Ltd.

33. The fly's reply Ode to a bullfrog!

Quickly ♩ = 104—120

Bright and brave, quick and a - gile, whizz - ing through the air.

Blue and green, fast and fear - less, buzz - ing ev - 'ry - where.

Big and fat, mean and hun - gry, bull - frog looks at me. I'm

light and crisp, small and tas - ty... think I'd bet - ter flee! Buzz, whee!

© 2022 by Faber Music Ltd.

34. Light of the moon

© 2022 by Faber Music Ltd.

light up my smile so the whole world can see.

light up my smile so the whole world can see.

Smil-ing at the moon, wish-ing you were here, light-ing up the world with me.

35. Thinking back

© 2022 by Faber Music Ltd.

36. A dance for Dorian

Wistfully ♩= 84—92

All

Do - ri - an mi - nor's a ve - ry sad key,

mf

p

con Ped.

try not to cry as you play it to me.

f

f

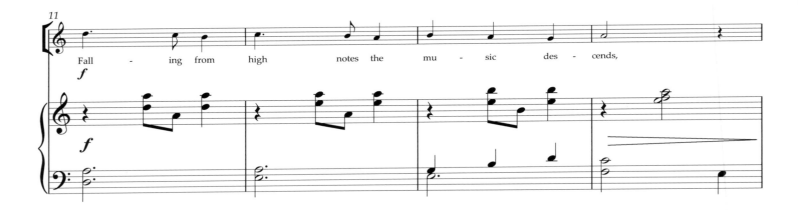

Fall - ing from high notes the mu - sic des - cends,

f

f

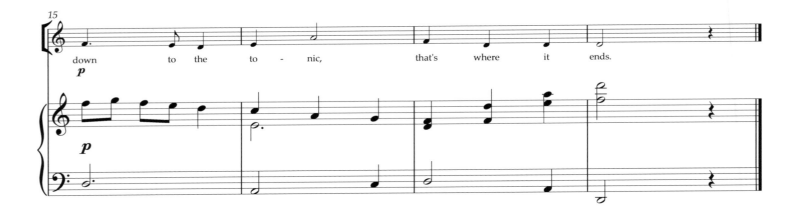

down to the to - nic, that's where it ends.

p

p

© 2022 by Faber Music Ltd.

37. Side by side

© 2022 by Faber Music Ltd.

38. What to do?

© 2022 by Faber Music Ltd.

D.S. al Fine*

* N.B. This instruction is D.C. al Fine in the instrumental parts.

39. Deep in the heart of the forest

© 2022 by Faber Music Ltd.

branch - es spread   so   thick - ly   that   dark - ness_ cloaks   the ground.
tall trees seem   to   ga - ther   a   cloak of_ si - lence   round.

40. Eggy soldiers!

Lyrics trad.

© 2022 by Faber Music Ltd.

All the king's hor - ses and all the king's men,

could - n't put Hump - ty to - ge - ther a - gain. Shame!

Ped.

41. Let shine your light

© 2022 by Faber Music Ltd.

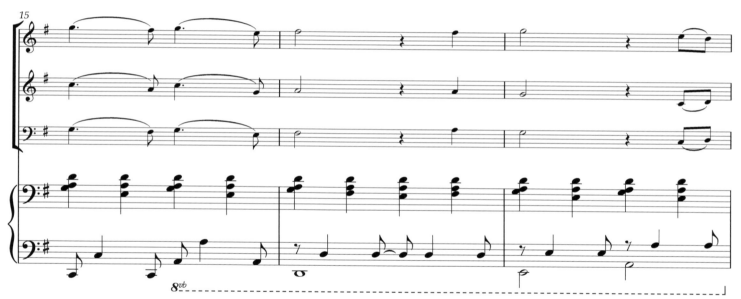

42. Flying

© 2022 by Faber Music Ltd.

43. Echo location

N.B. The key signature has been omitted for violin and double bass parts to avoid the use of B natural accidentals.

© 2022 by Faber Music Ltd.

44. Down in the dumps

N.B. The key signature has been omitted for violin and double bass
parts to avoid the use of B natural accidentals.

© 2022 by Faber Music Ltd.

45. Little waltz

© 2022 by Faber Music Ltd.

46. Far and near

With precision ♩ = 88

© 2022 by Faber Music Ltd.

47. Are you sure it's sharp?

© 2022 by Faber Music Ltd.

48. Back and forth

Vln.
Vla.
Cello

D. Bass

With feeling ♩ = 63—72

All Fs are sharp in this song, Cs are not, so don't go wrong!

con Ped.

D string's where F sharps all stay, A string has no sharps to play.

© 2022 by Faber Music Ltd.

49. Mini minuet

Dancing ♩ = 112—120

All

cresc.

© 2022 by Faber Music Ltd.

50. Spring into action

© 2022 by Faber Music Ltd.

51. Bowing free and easy

© 2022 by Faber Music Ltd.

N.B. **52. Dot and Spot** is unaccompanied.

53. Showtime!

© 2022 by Faber Music Ltd.

54. Twinkling waltz

© 2022 by Faber Music Ltd.

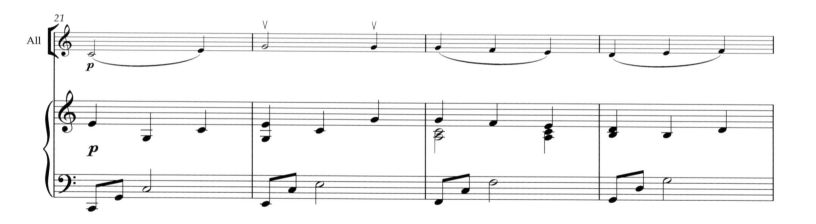

55. The pirates

© 2022 by Faber Music Ltd.

find the trea-sure, search-ing all a - round be - neath the ground, too rich to mea-sure, friends, we'll live a life of cheer!

Bad bow hold? You'll walk the plank, 'cause there's no mer-cy us pi-rates show! Good bow hold? Off we go!

56. Early one morning

Lyrics trad.

© 2022 by Faber Music Ltd.

57. Worm dance

© 2022 by Faber Music Ltd.

An overview of *Stringtastic Book 1*

Stringtastic Book 1 is split it into four distinct stages:

- **Stage 1: Tunes 1–15**
  This section follows on from *Stringtastic Beginners* by introducing notes on the G, C and E strings, plus further notes on the A string for the double bass. This section uses the same rhythms introduced in *Stringtastic Beginners* to allow students to focus on learning to play on the new strings.

- **Stage 2: Tunes 16–28**
  These tunes introduce new musical concepts based on the D major finger pattern covered in *Stringtastic Beginners*. Including dynamics, accents, slurs and new time signatures and rhythmic patterns.

- **Stage 3: Tunes 29–51**
  For the violin and viola, this section introduces low second fingers on all strings as well as changing between low and high second fingers. For the cello, this section introduces second fingers on all strings and changing between second and third fingers. For the double bass, there is more second finger practice and tunes for both the second and fourth fingers.

- **Stage 4: Tunes 52–57**
  This section brings everything together in pieces at Grade 1 (Early Elementary) standard.

Flexibility:

- Stage 1 can be started while students consolidate the first 20 D major duet tunes in *Stringtastic Beginners*.

- The different strings introduced at Stage 1 can be tackled in any order. There's no reason why the student can't tackle the E string tunes before the G string tunes – it's up to you!

- If you prefer to build upon the D major finger pattern before tackling the other strings, you can jump straight to Stage 2.

- You can choose to teach Stages 1 and 2 simultaneously: introduce the new strings in Stage 1, while building upon a D major finger pattern in Stage 2.

- Stage 3, like Stage 1, can be taught in any string order.

Ensembles:

- There are two duets without piano accompaniment in this book as well as several duets with piano accompaniment.

- The duets work for any combination of instruments, including string orchestras.

- As cellos and violas learn to play tunes on the C string, violins and double basses have their own workout. These sets of parts can be combined to create additional duets or string orchestra pieces. The same applies when violins and double basses learn to play on the E string, and at the point at which all instruments are dealing with flats and naturals (Stage 3).